A STRING OF PEARLS
UNSTRUNG

A STRING OF PEARLS UNSTRUNG

A THEOLOGICAL JOURNEY
INTO BELIEVERS BAPTISM

FRED MALONE

A String of Pearls Unstrung:

A Theological Journey into Believers' Baptism

© 1998 Founders Press. – First Edition

© 2022 Fred Malone – Revised Edition

Published by Founders Press
P.O. Box 150931 • Cape Coral, FL • 33915
Phone: (888) 525-1689
Electronic Mail: officeadmin@founders.org Website: www.founders.org

Printed in the United States of America

ISBN: 978-1-943539-30-7

Contents

Foreword

I was a young college student when I first read *A String of Pearls Unstrung*. Dr. Fred Malone's arguments, coupled with his gracious and personal manner of writing, helped keep me a Baptist. I had just finished wrestling with the doctrines of grace for several years and had finally concluded that the Bible teaches God's sovereignty in salvation. But then I began to struggle with what Scripture teaches about baptism because most of the authors who convinced me of my newfound Calvinistic soteriology were also Presbyterian in their ecclesiology. I was ready to be persuaded of paedobaptism, but I wanted to make sure I understood the arguments on both sides, and that's when I stumbled across Malone's pamphlet, which he narrates like a journal.

It persuaded me on a number of levels. First, it helped me to see key areas of hermeneutical inconsistency in Reformed paedobaptist theology. The most stark inconsistency is that the Reformed orthodox baptize the children of believers, but they will not allow those children to take the Lord's Supper, until they make a credible profession of faith. Yet Malone shows that in the old covenant, baby boys were circumcised and they were also allowed to take the Passover meal as soon as they could eat. Yet many Presbyterian theologians argue from New Testament priority that children may not partake of the Lord's Supper. They argue that the New Testament requires participants to examine themselves, and since young children are unable to obey that command, they may not take the Supper. But these same Presbyterian theologians do not allow the New Testament to determine who may be admitted to baptism. For me, that inconsistency exposed a weakness and arbitrariness in Reformed paedobaptist hermeneutical practice.

Second, Malone's work helped me begin to see that Jesus Christ fulfills the old covenant shadows. While Reformed paedobaptists think that old covenant circumcision is fulfilled in baptism and the Passover is fulfilled in the Lord's Supper, the Bible teaches that the old covenant types are fulfilled in Jesus Christ. Reformed paedobaptists also want to see a close correspondence between the mixed body of believers and unbelievers under the old covenant and the new covenant people. But Dr. Malone rightly argues that the old covenant people were actually a shadow of the true people of God, who are redeemed by the blood of Jesus. The only way to determine the nature of the new covenant people is to look to the revelation of the new covenant in Jeremiah 31 and Hebrews 8. Malone writes, "Christ is the Circumcision and Isaac of the Abrahamic Covenant. Christ is the Paschal Lamb and Annual Atonement for its continuation through Sinai. And Christ is the sole Mediator of the New Covenant fulfillment as the effectual sacrifice for all those considered 'in' the New Covenant, Christ's redeemed church. These redeemed ones—and only these—are the New Covenant participants."

Third, this booklet is not only an argument for credobaptism over and against paedobaptism, it also has blood and tears mixed with it. Malone was trained at a Presbyterian seminary and he served as a Presbyterian pastor for years before he came to Baptist convictions. He states the views of Reformed paedobaptist theology ever so carefully, but he also carefully and sincerely disassembles that position with the Word of God. Malone's change to Baptist ecclesiology cost him greatly. I observed too many Baptists becoming Presbyterians from what appeared to be convenience, but the depth of Malone's conviction earned my respect and made me take his arguments that much more seriously.

In God's good providence, I now have the joy of serving as the Senior Pastor at First Baptist Church of Clinton, Louisiana, where Fred is the Pastor Emeritus. I can tell you that he is still every bit as convinced of what he wrote in this pamphlet so many years ago. And it has been one of the great blessings of my life to serve alongside him in the kingdom of Christ. I encourage you to read this pamphlet carefully and share it with others, both Baptists and Reformed paedobaptists alike.

—Tom Hicks

First Baptist Church
Clinton, LA
July 18, 2022

Preface to the First Edition

This pamphlet is not intended to be a definitive work on baptism. Originally written in 1977, it is simply a journal I narrated for myself and for my friends who are interested in understanding why I moved from a paedo-baptist (infant baptism) position to a Baptist (disciples/confessors' baptism only) position. This journal has been edited for use as a booklet, but I have reserved a full revision for an upcoming book.

Any discussion about baptism, as with other doctrines in Scripture, is fruitless unless all parties are willing to sit down with open Bibles, open minds, and prayer-kept hearts. Infant baptism is an emotional issue because it involves our children and the promises of salvation to them. I simply ask that those who challenge my conclusions would sincerely and charitably study my arguments before they pass judgment.

It would have been easy to pass over this controversial topic and remain in the sphere of the Presbyterian Church. It still saddens my heart that my vows required me to withdraw myself voluntarily from that arena of service with its fellowship and opportunities. However, my conscience and practice must be ruled by Christ Himself through the guidance of His written Word and by no other man, tradition, or logical extension. Therefore, this journal sets forth what I understand to be His guidance of me through the Scriptures.

Stated briefly, as a covenant theologian I have come to believe that according to the Bible, the only proper subjects for Christian baptism are disciples of Christ. Jesus and His disciples were "making and baptizing more disciples than John" (John 4:1). First they became disciples, then they were baptized. Jesus and the apostles baptized people who had become believers ("disciples"). Further, the Great Commission commands to "make disciples of all nations [individuals from all nations, not the national entities], baptizing *them* [those who were made disciples, my emphasis] . . . teaching *them* [the disciples, my emphasis] to observe all that I have commanded you" (Matt. 28:19–20). This is exactly what happened at Pentecost. Only those who "received his [Peter's] word were baptized" (Acts 2:41), not infant children of believers. In the Westminster Confession and the Second London Baptist Confession, baptism and its subjects are included as elements of worship under the regulative principle of worship, positively instituted by God and "limited by His own revealed will".[1] The only form of baptism which fits this principle is that which was "instituted" and "prescribed in the Holy Scripture;" that is, baptism of disciples/confessors, not of infants.

Introduction

The greatest struggle in my theology has not been, oddly enough, the five points of Calvinism and the Reformed faith. I find these clear and well-defined from Genesis to Revelation. Rather, the thorn in my theological flesh has been baptism.

Although I was raised a Baptist, in seminary I came to the paedobaptist position because of several points of theology. These included the covenant with Abraham, the relationship between circumcision and baptism, the supposed disjunction between John's and Jesus' baptisms and Christian baptism, the argument of silence, the proof-texts concerning children in the covenant, and the testimony of tradition. The work which influenced me most was John Murray's *Christian Baptism*.

As I look back to those days as a sincere and searching seminary student I often wonder if I was as honestly searching for the truth as I thought I was. For in the hard crucible of sometimes bitter rejection by my Baptist friends over the doctrines of sovereign grace, and in the warm fellowship of my like-minded paedobaptist brethren, it is more than possible that I allowed subjective feelings to influence my interpretation of the objective truth about baptism. I do not believe that I am the only Baptist who became a Presbyterian under these circumstances. In fact, I believe many Baptists, frustrated with doctrinal shallowness, have left Baptist churches to find a theologically comfortable home in sound Presbyterian churches. However, the sacraments are never minor issues of doctrine, and it is my hope that this pamphlet will persuade many to stay in, help reform, and build more sound Baptist churches.

In any case, after graduation I reexamined my position on infant baptism and found many inconsistencies that, for whatever reasons, I did not find in seminary. I have attempted to let most of my work be as original as possible. However, two books which helped me verbalize many things already discovered are *Should Infants Be Baptized?*, by T. E. Watson, and *The Children of Abraham*, by David Kingdon. I highly recommend these works to my paedobaptist and Baptist friends.

I have dealt only with the proper subjects of baptism because I believe this to be the most important factor with which to begin. John Calvin himself believed that the Bible teaches immersion and that the early church practiced immersion.[2] I accept Calvin's analysis though he allowed diverse practices.

As I cover each point of theology in an informal narrative fashion, I hope to give glory to God by letting His infallible

Word be the absolute and final authority for each conclusion. My continual prayer is for the Holy Spirit to illumine my mind and the mind of the reader as we gaze together into the mind of God as revealed in the written Word.

THE THORN

The change to Baptist convictions began as I was reading Exodus 12 as part of my devotional exercises. Surely I had read it many times before, but this time a question pestered my soul. In the institution of the Passover feast, I read: "And you shall observe this rite as a statute for you and for your sons *forever* [emphasis added]" (Ex. 12:24). My question concerned the participation of the children in the feast, which is a foreshadowing of the Lord's Supper. And if they did participate, at what age did they begin? Further, what does this have to say about children's participation in the Lord's Supper? As I meditated, I wondered if this might not be simply a command to continue the ordinance from parent to child in unbroken generations. Therefore, I decided to research the point for a clearer understanding.

I concluded that the text can favor the participation of the household children of any age in the feast as well as be a command to continue the ordinance indefinitely. That the word "forever" implies the perpetuity of the ordinance is obvious. But in the covenant family context, the Hebrew *vav* conjunction ("and") seems to define the ordinance for all children of the household as well. The context seems to support this inclusion of the children in the meal because there were no other leavened breads and meats allowed to be present in the household (12:19–20, 28). With the exception of infants still on the breast, there was literally nothing left for the children to eat but the Passover meal! Some speculate that the children's question about the meal (v. 26) indicates their lack of participation in it. However, they certainly could have participated in the meal and even been able to ask the question about it long before they had the conceptual ability to understand its import.

I found it interesting how Berkhof and Murray differed regarding this situation, yet both disagreed with paedocommunion. Berkhof states:

> Children, though they were allowed to eat the passover in the days of the Old Testament, cannot be permitted to partake of the table of the Lord, since they cannot meet the requirements for worthy participation.[3]

While admitting that Old Testament children participated in the Passover, Berkhof excludes them from the Lord's Supper because the New Testament prescribes self-examination and discerning the body.

Murray, on the other hand, discounts the interpretation that infants participated in the Passover for two reasons: (1) there is no mention of infants in the text, and (2) the diet was not suitable for infants. One problem with Murray's objections is that the same reasoning may be consistently applied to the silence concerning infants in household baptisms. Also, his contention is presumptuous, that the children were of an age to understand the meaning of the Passover when they asked what it meant. How many times have our own children asked questions about Christ or the Lord's Supper and were not able to understand the answers? Further, Murray does not recognize that children are capable of ingesting both unleavened bread and meat as infants before one year of age.[4]

Therefore, I conclude from the text, context, and supporting Reformed comment that the children of the household who were capable of ingesting meat and unleavened bread partook of the Passover feast simply by their Old Covenant position in the household.

What are the implications of this fact? It amazed me that I ran across an article in the *Open Letter* the next month (1977), using this same fact for the basis of "Covenant Children's" communion. This publication by the Covenant Fellowship of Presbyterians printed an article by the pastor of Canal Street Presbyterian Church in New Orleans, advocating the passage of the P.C.U.S. amendment allowing baptized infant children entrance to the Lord's Table as soon as they are able to take the elements! The argument was based upon the transformation of circumcision into infant baptism as the principle for transforming the subjects of the Passover into the subjects of the Lord's Supper.

As I began to assimilate and analyze this article, several arguments against its conclusions came to mind. The two clearest were that (1) there is the scripturally-instituted command to examine oneself before participating, and (2) there is no positive command to include infants and small children in the supper. The first is an argument of precept according to the regulative principle of Scripture, and the second an argument of silence and inference. Both arguments seem to limit participation in the Lord's Supper observance to baptized disciples who are capable of understanding the meaning of the supper and are able to examine their inward spiritual motivation when taking it. I concluded, along with most Reformed theologians, that these two arguments are sufficient to show the error of infant or covenant communion.

What now is my point? Simply this: Why is New Testament regulation sufficient to define the subjects of the Lord's Supper but not infant baptism? Assuming that household children in the Old Covenant administration were allowed to participate in the Passover feast as soon as they were able to consume the elements, and assuming that household children in the New Covenant administration are not allowed to participate until professing faith and self-examination are evidenced, my questions are:

* What has changed in the application of the covenant family concept from the Old Covenant to the New Covenant?

* Why does the household child participate in the Passover and not in the Lord's Supper?

* Has the New Covenant child of believers less blessings than the household Old Covenant child?

* What exactly *are* the covenant blessings for the New Covenant household child, if any?

THE STRING OF PEARLS

While I recognized disagreement concerning the conclusion that the Old Covenant children participated in the Passover by covenant position, there remained in my mind a growing desire to reexamine the biblical basis for infant baptism. I thought that perhaps God was guiding me to restudy the doctrine so that I might be confirmed in my own mind that earlier in seminary I had not let subjective influences guide my search for objective truth. However, I reasoned that if I came to be a Baptist I had nothing to lose in accepting God's truth in the Word. Either way, I would be stronger in the end.

While all paedobaptist covenant theologians that I have read heartily agree that there is no positive command to baptize covenant infants, they cite what can appear to be an impressive number of individual pearls which can be strung together as a beautiful and unified necklace. This is the principle of hermeneutics called "good and necessary inference." John Murray has stated this principle for infant baptism:

> One of the most persuasive objections and one which closes the argument for a great many people is that there is no express command to baptise infants and no record in the New Testament of a clear case of infant baptism.... The evidence for infant baptism falls into the category of good and necessary inference, and it is therefore quite indefensible to demand that the evidence required must be in the category of express command or explicit instance.[5]

The problem with this statement is that it allows Old Testament inference from the Abrahamic Covenant to overrule the clearer and final New Testament fulfillment, prescription, and institution by revelation. According to Murray, one would have to present a command or example against infant baptism to overrule his Old Testament inference, even if it was never practiced. This is an absurd position hermeneutically.

The principle of "good and necessary inference" is legitimately used to support the cessation of such things as written revelation and modern day apostles. Yet in these cases, the basis for such inference is always New Testament revelation, not Old Testament implication. "The New is in the Old concealed; and the Old is in the New revealed" is an agreed upon hermeneutic which places more authority upon New Testament institution than upon Old Testament inference.

There may be an impressive collection of pearls strung upon the string of "good and necessary inference," yet both T. E. Watson and Herman Hoeksema (*Believers and Their Seed*) have aptly demonstrated that there is enough disagreement among covenant paedobaptist theologians on each specific pearl to warrant a reexamination of the "good and necessary inference" which strings them all together. Since this is a brief journal, I will simply use Watson's well-documented book (*Should Infants Be Baptized?*) to show that there is serious disagreement regarding specific Scriptures among major Reformed theologians on almost every point and ground supporting infant baptism.

What then are the pearls on the string? Since I am dealing with my own acceptance of paedobaptism, here are the pearls whose beauty caused me to add them to my string:

1. The covenant theology of the Old and New Testaments
2. The relationship between circumcision and baptism
3. The proof-texts concerning baptism
4. Jesus' attitude toward the children
5. The sanctification of believers' children
6. The disjunction of the baptism of John's and Christian baptism
7. The argument of silence
8. The argument of expanded blessings
9. The testimony of tradition

I have not dealt with mode in this journal because the issue of the biblical subjects of baptism is a far more important one.

1

THE FIRST PEARL

COVENANT THEOLOGY
IN THE OLD AND NEW TESTAMENTS

The primary basis for the baptism of the covenant child is claimed to be found in God's promise of covenant blessing to Abraham and to his "offspring." Abraham was justified by faith through believing in God's promises to be his God and to make him the father of many nations (Gen. 12–17; Rom. 4). He and his "offspring" would inherit Canaan as an everlasting possession. And, most important of all, the Lord promised to be the God of Abraham and of his "offspring." Then God granted the sign of this covenant, circumcision, to Abraham and to his "offspring" forever. This sign was also to be administered to all males in the household, born and bought. Since Abraham is called "the father of us all" (Rom. 4:16), and since Christians are

11

referred to as "Abraham's offspring" (Gal. 3:29) and "heirs according to the promise," it seems "good and necessary" to infer that the sign of New Testament baptism should be applied to the children of Abraham's "offspring" of faith as circumcision was applied to the children of Abraham's "offspring" of flesh (Col. 2:11–12). This is a compelling pearl for infant baptism.

THE COVENANT PARTICIPANTS

Several questions, however, must be put to this conclusion. First, if Christians, Jewish or Gentile, are the "offspring" of Abraham, should we both claim physical Canaan as our rightful territory and "everlasting" possession as well? Second, if circumcision is a "forever" sign of the Abrahamic Covenant, then why do the New Covenant "offspring" of Abraham not continue circumcision as a religious act? And, third, should Christians baptize not only infants but also all males bought or born into their homes?

It has often been objected that it is not legitimate to identify both children and physical land in the same category concerning the covenant promises to Abraham. I quite agree. However, what about the 318 male servants of the household of Abraham who were circumcised by virtue of their being in Abraham's household? How does this aspect of *people* in the covenant household, not *land*, apply in the New Covenant application of the Abrahamic Covenant?

There was a theological question concerning slaves' baptism in the pre-Civil War South among Presbyterians.

Meredith Kline attempts to deal with this issue of the application of covenantal household authority in the New Covenant administration of the Abrahamic Covenant in his book, *By Oath Consigned.*[6] However, Kline is unclear about whether or not the baptism of slaves is a legitimate application in the New Covenant administration. He shies away from saying that this practice is legitimate because of the silence of the New Testament and the difficulty of church discipline.[7] On the other hand, in the same paragraph, he seems to allow the plausibility of servant baptism in certain mission situations for temporary cultural expediency. The decision seems to be left to the individual covenant head in his application of the principles of culture, family, and church to his particular situation. The question of what is the scriptural way of handling one's slaves in this regard is really not answered. Are covenant theology and the New Covenant participant so loosely defined?

Along with most covenant theologians, I conclude that these land and servant elements of the Abrahamic Covenant do not presently apply to the New Testament Christian and church since Christ's kingdom is "not of this world" nor is it a theocratic nation, yet is still the "Israel of God" (Gal. 6:16). Most of us believe that Christians will possess Canaan in the New Heavens and the New Earth but not in the present administration of things. Nor do any seriously believe in servant baptism.

It must be understood that just because there was an inter-mixture of physical and spiritual elements in the Abrahamic

Covenant, it does not follow by implication that the same elements apply to the New Covenant. We all know that one became a member of the Abrahamic Covenant by physical circumcision, but God also called Abraham's seed to spiritually circumcise their hearts as well (Deut. 10:16). That the New Covenant emphasizes a spiritual circumcision does not automatically imply that there must be physical members in the New Covenant without such a heart. As Pastor Walter Chantry of Grace Baptist Church, Carlisle, Pennsylvania, has well said, "In the Old Covenant, all that was spiritual was identified with an outward nation. In the New Covenant, all that is outward is identified with a spiritual nation."[8] Therefore, those who apply the Abrahamic inclusion of physical children to the New Covenant as a basis for the infant baptism of the Christian's children must also honestly deal with the "forever" implications of Canaan, circumcision, and household adult membership in the New Covenant as well. There is too much inconsistency here to make a valid argument.

Therefore, the main question for me is: how does the Scripture apply the Old Testament promises which are given to Abraham and his "offspring" to the New Covenant fulfillment in the Christian and the church? Continuing, for the moment, to assume that baptism is the New Covenant counterpart of circumcision, let us define from Scripture the essence of the New Covenant and who exactly are the "offspring" of Abraham who should receive the New Covenant sign and blessings.

THE NEW COVENANT DESCRIBED

One of the key passages that must be considered in defining the meaning of the New Covenant is Jeremiah 31. In vv. 27–30, God declares that after the prophesied captivity each man will bear the responsibility for his own spiritual condition before God in a new way. Continuing this change of emphasis to individual responsibility in vv. 31–34, God defines a new basis for covenant membership and blessing in the New Covenant which is different from the basis for membership and blessing in the Old Covenant. In contrasting the Old and New Covenants, God's definition of the difference is that of heart renewal in each and every member of the New Covenant.

Initially, to become a participant in the Abrahamic Covenant and its continuation at Sinai, one simply had to be born into the physical descent of Abraham. Physical membership in this covenant was signified by circumcision, but one was cut off from the salvation of the covenant if he did not circumcise his heart as well (Deut. 10:16). However, it is important to note that many whose hearts were never circumcised continued to participate in visible Israel. Yet they were not visibly cut off from God's covenant people. Thus, the doctrine of the faithful remnant within physical Israel arose in the prophets (Jer. 23:1–6; 31:7). This remnant would come to fruition and fulfillment during the reign of "a Branch of righteousness" from David's line. It is this faithful remnant which is raised up in the days of the New Covenant (Jer. 31:7, 32–34).

Participation in the New Covenant, which is "not like" the Old Covenant, is defined as experiencing the reality of heart-religion in each and every member (Jer. 31:33–34). The New Covenant does not just introduce new blessings. Rather, all New Covenant members actually have the Law written on their hearts ("I will put My law within them, and I will write it on their hearts"), receive the forgiveness of sins ("I will forgive their iniquity, and I will remember their sin no more"), and know the Lord ("for they shall all know me, from the least of them to the greatest, declares the Lord").

This definition says nothing of participation in the New Covenant blessings by physical descent alone. Rather, the participants whom Jeremiah describes are the true "Israel" (Gal. 6:16). They are "the children of the promise," a faithful remnant according to God's "election of grace" (Rom. 9:6–8) in which every true member knows the Lord. This New Covenant in which God writes His Law on the heart of each one in the covenant is also defined in Ezekiel 36:24–28 as the time when God puts His Spirit within and gives a new heart that will be careful to observe His ordinances. This promise of the Spirit is also spoken to the whole house of Israel, indicating that this new heart will be evident in the nation as a whole. In fact, Galatians 3:14, 29 defines the fulfillment of the promise to Abraham in the New Covenant as the gift of the Spirit to all his "offspring," i.e., Jewish and Gentile believers (Rom. 4; see also the explanation of the promise in Acts 2:39 below).

Paedobaptist theologian, Herman Ridderbos, believes that Jesus' teaching on the kingdom of God and its born again members is "determined by the idea of the covenant." Jesus' reference to the New Covenant of Jeremiah 31 at the Last Supper affirms this understanding. Thus, the idea of God's people takes on a more restricted meaning in the New Covenant:

> God's people are those for whom Christ sheds his blood of the covenant. They share in the remission of sins brought about by him and in the unbreakable communion with God in the new covenant that he has made possible . . . In the light of the whole gospel they are the people who have accepted the preaching of the gospel in faith and conversion. It is they, *and no one else* (italics mine), who receive the salvation of the kingdom. They are "Israel," "God's people," and it is to them that all the promises of the covenant apply.[9]

Therefore, based upon Jeremiah 31:31–34 and its description of regeneration in the New Covenant participants, and in light of Christ's definition of the entrance requirements to the kingdom (John 3:5–6) and church (Matt. 16:16–18), I cannot say that children of believers are "in" the New Covenant or church or kingdom or "God's people" until they show, by outward confession, evidence of regeneration.

It has been objected that perhaps Jeremiah 31:34 is an eschatological reference because of the stated lack of need for anyone to teach his neighbor and brother. Therefore, the argument goes, this describes the church triumphant. Do we not need to teach each other in the New Covenant? Of course! But in addressing Israel, God is referring to neighbors and brothers in the New Covenant Israel! There is no need to evangelize the participants in the New Covenant because they all know the Lord! Of course we teach each other to observe all that Christ commanded us (Matt. 28:18–20). But there is no need to teach those in the New Covenant to "know the Lord" because they already know Him, having been taught by God Himself (John 6:44–45; 1 John 2:27; 1 Thess. 4:9). For this reason, the "least to the greatest" of those in the New Covenant are greater than John the Baptist, who was regenerated in the womb (Matt. 11:11). Therefore, I am not willing to concede that a believer's child is automatically in the New Covenant and is thereby greater than John the Baptist, until he/she shows evidence of regeneration by a profession of faith in Christ. Even if our Sovereign God were to regenerate children of believers in the womb, they should not be considered "in" the New Covenant until they show the evidence of regeneration by repentance and faith. This is the uniform command and example of the New Testament, and it precedes New Covenant baptism.

The New Covenant Sacrifice

To say that all physical infants of believers are "in" the New Covenant as the infants of Abraham were "in" the Abrahamic and Sinaitic Covenants violates the doctrine of particular redemption. Hebrews 9 reminds us that God's covenant requires mediation through blood. The Passover Lamb brought physical deliverance for all Israel because all ate it. The Annual Atonement (Lev. 16) was offered on behalf of the whole assembly, all Israel. Of course, these sacrifices could not cleanse the conscience, but their design was for the covenant people of God in the Old Testament. If Christ's sacrifice is offered up only for His elect people as the "New Covenant in My blood" (Luke 22:20; Mark 14:24), how can the unregenerate children of believers be said to be "in" the New Covenant, church, and kingdom without an effectual Mediator? They cannot. Indeed, Hebrews 9:15 defines Christ as an effectual Mediator of the New Covenant to insure that "those who are called may receive the promised eternal inheritance." Can one be said to be "in" the New Covenant or church without a Mediator? Not on the basis of the concept of the church in the New Testament. Though all would agree that false professors were addressed as members of the church for which Christ's effectual blood was shed, yet they were so addressed on the basis of their profession, not on the basis of their parents' faith. Even then, they were to be put out of the church if their profession proved spurious by their life. Yet there was some outward evidence to designate them "in" the church. But there is no clear basis for saying infants of believers are "in" the church unless we are also willing to say that they are "in" the "church of God which He obtained with His own blood" (Acts 20:28). No, if an infant is said to be "in" the New Covenant administration of the one covenant of grace and "in" the church without effectual mediation, severe violence is done to the biblical truth that "Christ loved the church and gave Himself up for her" (Eph. 5:25) Can an unregenerate infant be called "in" the church by Christ's effectual mediation and never receive salvation? Absolutely not. Therefore, violence is done to the doctrine of particular redemption.

The covenant of grace requires the blood of an effectual Mediator. Christ is the Circumcision and Isaac of the Abrahamic Covenant. Christ is the Paschal Lamb and Annual Atonement for its continuation through Sinai. And Christ is the sole Mediator of the New Covenant fulfillment as the effectual sacrifice for all those considered "in" the New Covenant, Christ's redeemed church. These redeemed ones – and only these – are the New Covenant participants.

The Seed of Abraham

This brings us to the next question: exactly who are the "offspring" of the Abrahamic Covenant who should receive the New Covenant counterpart of circumcision? In Romans 4, where Abraham is called "the father of us all," we find that God has fulfilled His promise to him to become the father of many nations by defining his "offspring" as those who are "of the faith of Abraham" (v. 16). Whether they are uncircumcised or circumcised, his "offspring" are those who "walk in the footsteps of the faith that our father Abraham had before he was circumcised" (vv. 11–12). There is no mention of the physical descendants of believers as included in the New Covenant fulfillment of the Abrahamic Covenant; rather, it is only those who actually have obtained "the righteousness of faith" by receiving Jesus Christ (cf. John 1:12–13).

In Galatians 3, Paul clearly indicates that physical descent and circumcision have no necessary relationship to the fulfillment of the Abrahamic Covenant in the New Covenant. The promises of the Abrahamic Covenant were made to Abraham and to his one "offspring," named Christ (3:16). Therefore, the New Covenant fulfillment of the promise to make Abraham the father of many nations is through Christ – his fulfilled "offspring" – and all who have faith in Him. The actual definition of the Abrahamic "offspring" is "those who are of faith" (vv. 7, 9). If you belong to Christ, then you are Abraham's "offspring," "heirs according to promise" (v. 29). The only definition of the "offspring" of Abraham in the New Covenant is Christ and His "offspring" who have experienced the reality of saving faith, i.e., the Abrahamic promise of the Spirit (vv. 14, 29).

Who is the "offspring" of Christ to whom belong the promises of the Abrahamic Covenant? It is those who belong to Christ (Gal. 3:29) and those alone, revealed by their faith. The only ones who have a claim to the inheritance of God are the children of God by the Spirit's regeneration (Rom.8:9, 14–17; John 1:12–14). Therefore, no one is considered an inheritor of the Abrahamic promises until by faith he becomes a "offspring" of Abraham through Christ, who is the literal fulfillment of Abraham's "offspring." And we "belong to Christ" only through the faith that evidences regeneration (Gal. 3:22, 29).

Also, if we continue to assume that baptism is the counterpart of circumcision, we are faced with the problem of verse 27 where all (without distinction between infants and adults) who were baptized into Christ have clothed themselves with Christ. It is only prejudice that keeps one from defining this in terms of water baptism.[10] Paul is alluding to their experience of union with Christ, symbolized by their confirming experience of water baptism. No one would claim that all the participants in the Old Covenant circumcision experienced the reality of saving faith. Nor would anyone claim that all who receive disciples' baptism have saving faith. Yet the New Covenant fulfillment of the Abrahamic promise is an "offspring" consisting of all who are "of faith," who receive the Abrahamic promise of the Spirit, and who confess their faith through baptism as the outward sign.

The Abrahamic Covenant was entered by circumcision; the New Covenant is entered by faith in Christ. Only Abraham's New Covenant "offspring" of faith should receive the New Covenant sign of baptism.

Now, you may be thinking, Does this really say anything that actually prohibits the giving of the covenant sign of baptism to the children of Abraham's New Covenant "offspring"? Before I answer that question, let us first examine the Scriptures to determine the significance of circumcision in relation to the New Covenant.

2

THE SECOND PEARL

Circumcision is the second pearl on the string of "good and necessary inference." What exactly is the counterpart of circumcision in the New Covenant? Is it water baptism? What exactly does the Scripture say about the implications of circumcision in the New Covenant?

Physical Circumcision and Heart Circumcision

In Romans 2:28–29, we find that circumcision was always meant to represent the inward work of the Spirit on the heart. According to the principles of typological interpretation, physical circumcision is the type and regeneration is the antitype or fulfillment. This was the definition of a true Jew, whether of Jewish or Gentile descent. The outward sign of circumcision was to symbolize that which God desired inwardly of the heart. But more than that, the reality of the symbol also had to be present in order for a person to be a true Jew or to receive all of God's covenant blessings.

This same truth is taught in Romans 9:6–8, where Paul says that "not all who are descended from Israel belong to Israel." This is another reference to the faithful remnant idea which began in the physical nation of Abraham's descendants and came to fruition in the New Covenant members or church. This is further explained in Romans 4:12, where the promised "offspring" of Abraham consists not of those of physical descent only, but those who are of the *faith* of their father Abraham. These, and these only, are his fulfilled "offspring" (Rom. 4:23). It is those who are of faith, Jew and Gentile, who are the "offspring" of Abraham. In all these Scriptures, the true Jews, or Abraham's "offspring," in fulfillment of God's promise to him, are those who have the circumcision of the heart by the Spirit, which is exhibited by faith in Christ.

Heart Circumcision and Baptism

What then is the counterpart of circumcision in the New Covenant? The most quoted text to link circumcision and water baptism is Colossians 2:9–12:

> For in him the whole fullness of deity dwells bodily, and you have been filled in him, who is the head of all rule and authority. In him also you were circumcised with a circumcision made without hands, by putting off the body of the flesh, by the circumcision of Christ,

> having been buried with him in baptism, in which you
> were also raised with him through faith in the power-
> ful working of God, who raised him from the dead.

This text, however, has been misinterpreted by many covenant paedobaptists.

Paul teaches that all Christians have received circumcision
by the circumcision of Christ. What is "the circumcision
of Christ?" It may be interpreted to be either the death
of Christ objectively or the circumcising of the believer's
heart by Christ. Either way, Paul is speaking of the manner
in which the believer has been "circumcised also" through
Christ's death and resurrection. Because of Christ's death,
we have received a better circumcision than the Judaizers
"by putting off the body of the flesh, . . . buried with him
in baptism, in which you also were raised with him *through
faith* [emphasis added] in the powerful working of God,
who raised him from the dead."

Here is a definite link between circumcision and baptism.
Christians have been circumcised "also" by being buried with
Christ in baptism. But is Paul referring only to the actual
water baptism as the direct fulfillment of circumcision? To
quote Paul, "Certainly not!" This fulfilled circumcision is
"made without hands." There is no human hand involved
in its administration, whether by knife or by water. His full
definition of the Christian's fulfillment of circumcision is
"by putting off the body of the flesh, by the circumcision of
Christ, having been buried with him in baptism, in which
you also were raised with him *through faith* [emphasis

added] in the powerful working of God, who raised him from the dead."

To summarize, the Christian's circumcision is that union with Christ's death and resurrection, symbolized by baptism, which is evidenced by outward faith! Verses 13 and 14 also support this view by defining the ones who have received the "circumcision" as those who have actually experienced the new birth and the blotting out of sins. This new life of faith is the New Covenant heart-circumcision "by the circumcision of Christ" which fulfills the type of Old Covenant circumcision. Only these people were "buried with Christ in baptism," according to this passage, because their hearts had been circumcised; and this was exhibited by their faith. Their water baptism symbolized their prior spiritual baptism.

Some paedobaptists consider union with Christ in baptism in Romans 6:3–4 as a *secondary* reference to water baptism, counting it primarily as a reference to regeneration. Yet, inconsistently, they use the same concept of union with Christ in baptism in Colossians 2:11–12 as a *primary* reference to the relationship of water baptism to circumcision instead of its clear intention of relating circumcision to regeneration. My conclusion is that Paul defined the circumcision of Christians in Colossians 2:9–12 as primarily union with Christ by faith, secondarily symbolized in their water baptism, as in Romans 6:3–4.

If circumcision is the sign and seal of the Abrahamic Covenant, what then is its New Covenant counterpart? I believe the Scriptures define it to be the circumcision of the heart by the Spirit exhibited in faith. This is why Paul prohibited physical circumcision. They had received its reality in the new heart (Gal. 3:3). Paul tells the Galatians that they do not need physical circumcision to enter into the covenant relationship with God because they have already entered that covenant relationship by the circumcision of Christ, a new heart by union with His death and resurrection. Therefore, as circumcision (the shadow or type) was the sign of entrance into the Abrahamic Covenant and the seal of Abraham's saving faith, so regeneration (the form or antitype) is the sign of entrance into the New Covenant and the seal of the believer's faith (Eph. 1:13–14; John 3:5–6).

Baptism then, is the *indirect* fulfillment of physical circumcision only through its association with the *direct* fulfillment, spiritual circumcision. This is why we see only confessors' baptism in the New Testament record. It was easy to know who entered the Abrahamic Covenant; they were born into the household and were outwardly circumcised. But how can one tell if someone has entered the New Covenant and has experienced spiritual circumcision? Only by his repentance and faith, signified by the outward sign of fulfilled circumcision and cleansing, water baptism. Acts 2:37–42 is clear exegetical proof that the only children baptized were those who received Peter's word of repentance and faith in Christ (Acts 2:38–41). They outwardly showed inward circumcision and then were baptized. This is how Christ ordained to build His church (Matt. 16:16–18; 28:19).

Water baptism, then, is the outward sign of the inward circumcision of the heart rather than the outward counterpart of the outward circumcision of the flesh. Just as Abraham's Old Covenant "offspring" initially entered the covenant by physical circumcision and confirmed it by spiritual circumcision, his New Covenant "offspring" initially enter the covenant by spiritual circumcision and confirm it by baptism. Physical descendants of Abraham's New Covenant "offspring" are not to be permitted the sign of baptism until they show by faith that they have also become the spiritual "offspring" of Abraham. David Kingdon's book, *Children of Abraham*, is a more thorough study of this concept. Regeneration by the Spirit, not the infant baptism of believers' "offspring," is the fulfillment of the promise to give a multitude of nations to Abraham as his descendants. Faith comes first as the evidence of regeneration, then comes baptism; not the other way around.

3

THE THIRD PEARL

Having concluded thus far that Abraham's New Covenant "offspring" consists solely of those "of faith" and the Spirit, and that the circumcision of the New Covenant is not Abraham's but Christ's circumcision in regeneration, evidenced by faith and outwardly symbolized by baptism, let me now deal with the pearl of specific proof-texts which have been used to support the baptism of covenant children.

ACTS 2:39

"For the promise is to you and to your children, and to all who are afar off, as many as the Lord our God will call."(NKJV) This is a pivotal text for infant baptism. Paedobaptists like Berkhof, Murray, and Marston sometimes cut the text off at "the promise is to you and to your children," exclaiming that these Jews immediately assumed the covenant sign of baptism was for their children. However, the text also includes "those who are afar off, as many as the Lord our God will call." Two things must be defined in this text: (1) what is the "promise," and (2) who is to receive it?

First, the word *epaggelia* (promise) in v. 39 is used in the context to identify the promise of the Holy Spirit through Christ's mediation, evidenced outwardly through repentance and faith (v. 38; see also Luke 24:49; Acts 1:4; and Acts 2:33). If one points out that these were Jews who would immediately think of the promise to Abraham and his "offspring," he would be right. For we find that the "promise" to Abraham included the pouring out of the Spirit on his "offspring," Jew and Gentile (Gal. 3:14), given only to those who believe (Gal. 3:22).

Going further, we are heirs according to the "promise" and Abraham's seed if and only if we belong to Christ (Gal. 3:14, 29). Romans 4:16 states that the "promise" to Abraham is made certain to each and every "offspring" of Abraham – Jew and Gentile – by faith, that it may be in accordance with grace and not the flesh. Romans 9:6–8 declares that it is only the children of the "promise" (i.e., regenerated by the Holy Spirit) who are regarded as Abraham's "offspring" and the true Israel. And this is in the context of sovereign election, which determines who receives the "promise," even within the covenant family of Isaac.

To briefly summarize, the "promise" made to Abraham that he would become "the father of many nations" is fulfilled in the New Covenant by the certain pouring out of the promised Spirit upon his "offspring" who come to God through repentance and faith in the perfect mediation of Jesus Christ. Only those who receive the "promise" of the Spirit through repentance and faith in Christ are actually Abraham's "offspring" and "heirs." These alone are entitled to the sign of the New Covenant, which is baptism.

Again, who is offered the promise of the Spirit through repentance and faith in Christ in Acts 2:38? All those mentioned in v. 39, "you and to your children and to all those who are afar off." But is this an indiscriminate assurance that each of those mentioned will definitely receive the promise? No. Only "as many as the Lord our God will call." Here is the condition for receiving the promise: the effectual calling of God.

The real question is, to whom does *hosous an* (as many as) refer? Does *hosous an* (as many as) refer only to "those afar off" (usually understood to be a reference to the Gentiles), or does it refer to the whole phrase, including "you and your children?" According to the Greek lexicon by Arndt and Gingrich, *hosous an* introduces a conditional relative clause which denotes the action of the verb as dependent upon some circumstance or condition. This is, namely, the sovereign will of God in effectual calling expressed in the subjunctive of *proskaleo* (may call). *Hosous* is the masculine accusative plural for the verb *proskaleo*. And since *teknois*, *humin*, and *pasin* (children, you and all) are collectively offered the promise by use of the conjunction *kai* (and), we may refer to these three dative plurals as the compound indirect object. Also, since *teknois* and *pasin* are masculine, *hosous an* (as many as) may legitimately modify both of them. Therefore, all three classes are offered the promise of the Spirit through repentance and faith. Yet, in *hosous an*, the condition of reception by all three must depend on the sovereign effectual calling of God. There is no greater promise to the children of those addressed than to the Jew and Gentile parents present. Not all those addressed received the promise and were baptized, but only those who "received" Peter's word of repentance and faith by God's effectual calling, including the children (2:41).

One objection to my line of reasoning is that there would be no need to mention "and your children" if they were given the same promise as their parents – they would have been included in the "you" which addresses the multitude. Therefore, the argument goes, the mention of "and your children" is evidence of the continuation of the covenant family concept and the application of the covenant sign upon one's children. However, the very mention of children as a separate category indicates that the apostle wanted to emphasize that there was no misunderstanding that they were not to receive baptism unless they repented and believed as verse 38 clearly requires. A second answer to this objection is that all those who were baptized partook of the Lord's Supper immediately afterward (v. 42). If infants were baptized with their parents, did they also partake of the breaking of bread? The objection does not stand.

Another common objection states that Acts 2:39 must first be read through the eyes of the Abrahamic Covenant. However, it is my belief that the fuller revelation of the New Covenant must define how the Abrahamic Covenant is fulfilled in it, rather than letting the Abrahamic Covenant interpret the New Covenant revelation of its fulfillment. It is a principle of interpretation that is in question here. We teach our children this principle by describing the relationship between the testaments with a little rhyme:

The New is in the Old concealed

The Old is in the New revealed.

Acts 2:38–39, and 41 support the principle that New Covenant revelation should define the participants of the New Covenant fulfillment of the Abrahamic Covenant rather than vice versa. Only those children in the crowd who received Peter's word were baptized. There is no other exegetical possibility in the text and context.

Regardless of their age, only those who received Peter's word and claimed God's promise were baptized. There is no mention in this passage of infants being baptized along with their parents. In fact, this passage explicitly hinges the reception of the promise of the Spirit upon God's sovereign effectual calling which is evidenced by repentance and faith. These and these only were baptized into the fellowship of the church.

Acts 2:39 defines the fulfillment of the "promise" only in those who are effectually called by God – those who receive the Word in repentance and faith. These only should be baptized.

The "Household Baptism" Texts

The question of household baptisms has long been used to support paedobaptism. These are the baptisms of the households of Cornelius, Lydia, the Philippian jailer, Stephanas, and Crispus.

Cornelius' Household (Acts 10:22; 11:12,14)

The account of Peter's preaching the gospel to Cornelius' household does not support infant baptism. Peter did preach the gospel to the whole household, and "all" the household was saved. How do we know that? Acts 10:44 and 11:15 state as much. The Holy Spirit fell upon them "all" and led them to repentance and faith (11:17–18). In fact, Peter explicitly stated in 10:47 that he baptized only those who "received the Holy Spirit as we did." This extension of Pentecost to the Gentiles clearly defined who was baptized. There is no mention of infants in the household, but only those who were "listening to the message" (10:44). Infants are capable of being regenerated by God (e.g., John the Baptist), and some may have been present. But they are not able to listen to the gospel and to "speak with tongues and magnify God" (Acts 10:46). Only the people who did this received baptism as a sign of the Abrahamic "promise" of the Spirit (Gal. 3:14). I conclude that the episode in

Cornelius' household not only does not support infant baptism but is also a strong indicator for disciples'/confessors' baptism.

Lydia's Household (Acts 16:15)

The case of Lydia is inconclusive. Where was Lydia's husband? She may not have been married at all. Only women are mentioned at the riverbank. And it appears that she and her household were baptized at the river before she took Paul back to her house. This opens the probability that only women were in her household (every member of which was probably at the riverbank with her) and that she was an unmarried or widowed businesswoman. Even if this is not entirely accurate, there is no mention of infants or older children in her household. Even many paedobaptists hold this instance of household baptism as inconclusive for their position.

Philippian Jailer's Household (Acts 16:30–34)

The account of the Philippian jailer is probably the best possibility for including infants in the household baptism. All his household was baptized, but it is wrong to apply the promise of verse 31 to the "covenantal baptism" of the household based upon the jailer's faith. This is clearly demonstrated in the following verses, where it is recorded that Paul and Silas preached the gospel to "all who were in his house" (v. 32) and that "all his household" (v. 34) believed in God with him.

There is a translation problem with this text that needs to be examined. J. A. Alexander (*Acts*) agrees that v. 31 is simply a promise of salvation by faith to the jailer and his household upon belief by both. Verse 34 is more complicated. The NASB, NIV, KJV, Williams, and Beck translations indicate that the faith which was shared by his whole household was the basis for their rejoicing: "having believed in God with his whole household." However, the participle is masculine, singular and seems to describe the faith of the jailer: "he rejoiced along with his entire household that he [the jailer] had believed in God." The emphasis seems to be that the household rejoiced with him because he had found faith (ESV, RSV, NEB).

Even if the latter interpretation is correct, we still have the problem of infants rejoicing. It is true that infants can detect and participate in joy in a household. But can infants rejoice because they realize their father has found faith in God? This may well be the basis for the whole household's rejoicing. However, because of the context in preaching the Word to all in the house and because all were resultantly baptized, I believe their rejoicing was the same as the jailer's rejoicing – the evidence of a new-found faith and redemption expressed in the joy of the Holy Spirit's regeneration. Because they all heard the gospel, were baptized, and rejoiced, it is a legitimate conclusion that they all believed. He and his "entire household" were baptized because they all believed. Can infants hear the Word and respond in faith? No. If infants were present, for which there is no proof, the context denies that they were baptized. In fact, the context suggests that no infants were present. This case of household baptism actually lends support to confessors' baptism.

Crispus' Household (Acts 18:8)

A related case which supports the same conclusion concerns the household of Crispus. Here is a definite account concerning baptism in which the whole household, along with Crispus, believed in the Lord. It should also be noted that in the same verse, the other Corinthians who were baptized had *first* believed. It seems clear that the whole household *first* believed and then were baptized. This case also positively supports confessors' baptism within households.

Stephanas' Household (1 Cor. 1:16)

The last household baptism mentioned in the New Testament is that of Stephanas by Paul. The thrust of this text is that the baptized believers were in division and controversy over who baptized them. It seems they were capable of knowing who baptized them, thus excluding infants. Further, 1 Corinthians 16:15 describes the "household of Stephanas" as having devoted themselves for ministry to the saints. Infants cannot self-consciously devote themselves in such a way. Yet even if this does not prohibit infants in the household of Stephanas, the most that can be said is that we do not know if infants were present. At best, this account is inconclusive for infant baptism.

In summary, the accounts of Lydia's and Stephanas' households are inconclusive, while the accounts of Cornelius', Crispus', and the jailer's households actually point to conscious belief and regeneration before baptism. Therefore, I conclude that the weight of the household baptisms leans toward confessors' baptism.

4

THE FOURTH PEARL

JESUS' ATTITUDE TOWARD CHILDREN

One set of proof-texts has often been used to point out that Jesus taught the inclusion of infants of believers in the covenant of grace. This is the group which shows Jesus with the children.

MATTHEW 18:1–10

The first set of passages consists of Matthew 18:1–10, Mark 9:33–37 and Luke 9:46–48. In each of these, Jesus set a little child before His disciples to teach them a lesson. The contextual problem was their arrogance in discussing which was the greatest disciple. In Matthew 18:2 we find that the *paidion* (little child) responded to Jesus' call in the verb *proskalesamenos* (having called to Himself). This is the same verb of Acts 2:39, which conditions the reception of God's promise through repentance and faith by God's effectual calling. This means that the child was not an infant and was capable of responding to Jesus' call.

In this context, Jesus taught His disciples three things. First of all, they must be converted and become "as little children" to enter the kingdom of heaven. The use of the child as an illustration of their needed humility is clearly preceded by the need of conversion to enter the kingdom of heaven (18:2–5). This passive use of *strepho* (to turn or change) lays down a requirement to enter the kingdom of heaven which is akin to the new birth in John 3. Their vain claims at greatness betrayed proud hearts.

Jesus defined what He meant in verse 3 by the inferential *oun* (therefore) of verse 4. They must be converted and humble themselves "like *this* child" to enter into and to be great in the kingdom of heaven. This little child came to Jesus at His call without regard to anything within himself; he came humbly.

Secondly, Jesus taught the disciples that they must receive even children who come to them as receiving Himself. They must honor the least among them as they would honor Christ Himself, instead of thinking themselves as greater (see Jer. 31:33–34; Matt. 11:11).

Thirdly, Jesus taught the disciples that to cause one of "these little ones who believe in me" to stumble was an offense against God and would bear His wrath. These passages have nothing to do with infants in the covenant because this *paidion* (little child) responded to Jesus' call, *proskaleo*, as a believer in Him. This childlike humble submission to Christ as Lord was what He was trying to teach His disciples regarding the attitudes and dispositions that characterize His kingdom. It is neither an instance of nor a support for infant baptism.

MATTHEW 19:13–15

A second set of passages has been appealed to more often as a support of infant covenant privileges in baptism: Matthew 19:13–15; Mark 10:13–16; and Luke 18:15–17. The disciples rebuked the people for bringing the little children to Jesus. In Luke 18:16 we read that Jesus called the children to Himself (*proskalesamenos*) "called them to him" (this is the same word found in Acts 2:39), just as He did in the previous set of passages. Then He commanded the disciples to quit restraining the children from coming to Him.

Although some have pointed out that Luke calls the children mentioned in this passage *brephe* (infants), yet the reflexive pronoun *auta* (them) defines those who were restrained from coming to Jesus as the *brephe*, not the parents who were bringing them. The context defines these "infants" as capable of responding to Jesus' call. Also, it should be pointed out that Paul reminded Timothy that he had known the Scriptures from a *brephous* (a babe), that is, from infancy. This shows that *brephe* may be used to describe a child who is old enough to learn the Scripture. Such a child certainly would be old enough to come to Jesus when called by Him.

The picture seems to be that the parents brought the children to be blessed, and then Jesus called the children to come to Him. The children who came to Him were picked up and blessed. Once again Jesus taught that one must "receive" the kingdom of God as a little child receives it to enter the kingdom. There is no promise here to these children unless they come to Jesus and receive the kingdom as well. In fact, if any passage in Scripture teaches the fallacy of paedobaptism, this one does. Neither Jesus nor His disciples baptized these children. Rather, the Lord blessed them.

In summary, Jesus did bless children as they were presented to Him by their parents. However, no promise of entrance into the kingdom is made to these children unless they also come to Jesus and receive the kingdom as examples of the way adults should receive it. The most that can be seen in these passages is infant blessing. There is certainly no hint of infant baptism.

5

THE FIFTH PEARL

THE SANCTIFICATION OF BELIEVERS' CHILDREN

To the rest I say (I, not the Lord) that if any brother has a wife who is an unbeliever, and she consents to live with him, he should not divorce her. If any woman has a husband who is an unbeliever, and he consents to live with her, she should not divorce him. For the unbelieving husband is made holy because of his wife, and the unbelieving wife is made holy because of her husband. Otherwise your children would be unclean, but as it is, they are holy. But if the unbelieving partner separates, let it be so. In such cases the brother or sister is not enslaved. God has called you to peace. For how do you know, wife, whether you will save your husband? Or how do you know, husband, whether you will save your wife? (1 Cor. 7:12–16).

First Corinthians 7:12–16 is a passage which is often used to illustrate the special position of believers' children "in" the church and covenant of grace and to argue for their right to baptism by physical line. However, there are at least two more credible explanations that would permit the children to be called "holy" and yet prevent their right to baptism until repentance and faith are evidenced.

First, the context of this particular passage has to do with a Christian who is married to an unbeliever. The whole context has to do with Christians remaining in the condition they are when saved (7:17–40). Should they remain married or should the Christian leave the unbeliever? Paul declares that they should remain married because God sanctifies the unbelieving partner. The whole of Scripture clearly establishes that the only way for anyone to be saved and thereby "sanctified" in this saving sense is by personal and saving belief in Christ. In this passage, however, Paul is using the term "sanctified" in the sense of receiving God's recognition of a legitimate marriage. This is the main point!

Paul's further point is that the children are not *akatharta* (unclean), but *hagia* (holy) in light of the unbelieving spouse's sanctification by their relationship to the believer. Many have seen this as a reference to the special position of believers' children with God. However, the context and usage of *akatharta* (unclean) must help define the sense of *hagia* (holy) here. The main thought concerns the recognition of the marriage by God. If the marriage were not accepted by God, then it would be illegitimate and unclean- and so would the children.

The only other use of *akatharta* in the New Testament in reference to a person is in Acts 10:28. There Peter told Cornelius, not yet a believer in Christ, that God had instructed him to consider no man *akatharta*. Although Cornelius was a God-fearer and might be called "holy" for the sake of the fathers (Rom. 11:16), yet he was not "holy" by virtue of being "in" the New Covenant thereby having a right to baptism. Here is one instance where a person was considered not unclean – and possibly "holy" for the sake of the fathers – yet not "in" the covenant of grace.

Therefore, both context and word study suggest that *hagia* (holy) refers to the legitimacy or sanctioning of the marriage and of the children rather than, necessarily, to the covenant promises of salvation and sanctification. Also, how old are the children of this legitimized marriage? Are they infants, teenagers, or adults? If this opens the way to covenant baptism, should all the children still living at home be considered *hagia* (holy) and baptized in the covenant relationship, even if adolescents or adults? Certainly not, according to the rest of Scripture on confessors' baptism. Any arbitrary attempts to define ages of accountability in order to limit baptism to minor children in this household also encounter problems. Esau was circumcised at age twelve, and Israelites up to age forty were circumcised by Joshua (Josh. 6). Neither one of these situations required a good confession before circumcision. If 1 Corinthians 7:14 prescribes baptism of "holy" children simply because of their physical descent, then even adult children should be included. In light of these difficulties, it is better to understand this passage as speaking of the children's legitimacy before God.

Second, there is an alternative to the legitimacy position which still does not include either spouse or child "in" the New Covenant.

The real question here is how can an unbelieving spouse be "sanctified," and how can the child of a believer be called "holy" under the New Covenant administration of grace? If the basic meaning of both of these words is "set apart" unto God, then further questions arise as to how each of the parties is "set apart" unto God and what the relationship of each is to the New Covenant.

Most agree that the unbelieving spouse is not in the New Covenant until regeneration (Acts 26:18). However, Kline has to be somewhat arbitrary in order to explain how the believing husband's marital covenantal authority has changed from including his wife in the Old Covenant while not including her in the New Covenant. Yet he maintains that the believing husband's parental covenantal authority is still valid in the New Covenant as the basis for his children being "in" the covenant and receiving baptism.[11] Such intricate logic is far too arbitrary to be convincing. Instead, it seems that by union with the believer, God recognizes the marriage as holy and promises to accept the unbeliever's husband or wife in "setting apart" that marriage to fulfill His purposes.

In the case of the children in this mixed marriage, the way in which they are "set apart" is more difficult to determine. Two texts often used to support the children's participation in the New Covenant fulfillment of the Abrahamic Covenant are Romans 11 and Ephesians 6:1–4. They deserve our consideration.

First, Paul states in Romans 11:16 that his kinsmen in the flesh, the branches presently cut off from participation in the olive tree of the New Covenant, are still "holy" because their root is "holy." However, these "beloved for the sake of their forefathers" (v. 28) shall be grafted in again if they do not continue in unbelief (v. 23). Here is the case of physical descendants of Abraham and his covenant promises (9:1–5) who are yet "holy" but not "in" the New Covenant and kingdom until they believe. Here is one use of "holy" applied to physical "offspring" who are outside the New Covenant because of their unbelief. This supports the view that the children of 1 Corinthians 7:14 can be considered "holy" for the sake of their parents and their heritage in the gospel blessings and yet not be "in" the New Covenant until they believe. Therefore, they may be considered "holy" as were the physical "offspring" of Abraham (Romans 11:16), yet be refused the covenant sign until they profess repentance and faith.

Secondly, if we strictly say (as many paedobaptists do) that the children of Ephesians 6:1–4 were addressed and accepted as saints (1:1), we also must strictly say that they had believed and were sealed with the Holy Spirit of promise (1:13). This is hardly a convincing argument concerning the inclusion of children in the church without regeneration and conversion. The fact that the children would be able to understand Paul's exhortation, were called saints, and were sealed by the Spirit, makes it perfectly plausible that he was talking to professing children who were real members of the New Covenant church.

However, it is also possible that Paul was addressing the children in the congregational gathering who sat under the preached Word of God even though they are not yet personally "in" the New Covenant church. Obedience to the fifth commandment is required of all children, believers and unbelievers alike. It is not uncommon for pastors to address churches as the "saints" when there is an unchurched child of unchurched parents in the assembly. Is Paul's exhortation inapplicable to them? Of course not. To appeal to Ephesians 6:1–4 as teaching that unbelieving children are members of the New Covenant and church is to "grasp at straws."

If we are going to make the children of Ephesians 6 members of the church, there is better evidence that they are considered believers and, therefore, have been baptized (Eph. 1:13; 4:4–6). The inadequate appeal to Ephesians only further supports the possibility that the children referred to may be considered "set apart" as privileged by their gospel heritage and exposure, yet not actually be "in" the New Covenant Church and entitled to baptism.

It is my conclusion that 1 Corinthians 7:14 is referring either to the children's legitimacy in the eyes of God, or at the most, to their "set apart" position for the sake of their parents' gospel heritage rather than covenant position. And how can we give two separate meanings to the sanctification of the children, on the one hand, and not to the unbelieving parent, on the other hand, unless we do so arbitrarily? It is impossible to do so except by a prejudicial treatment of the text. This verse makes no mention of covenant children's baptism even though this would have been a perfect opportunity for Paul to explain that practice to these Gentile

Corinthians. The use of this text to support infant baptism is completely unwarranted.

After examining the important pearl of prooftexts for infant baptism I come away with more doubt than proof. What I find with transparent honesty and clear conscience is that these prooftexts support believers' baptism much more than they do infant baptism.

6

THE SIXTH PEARL

THE DISJUNCTION OF JOHN'S AND
JESUS' BAPTISM WITH CHRISTIAN BAPTISM

There is often an attempt to differentiate the intent and subjects of John's and Jesus' baptisms and the intent and subjects of Christian baptism. This is an unbiblical and erroneous differentiation.

It is usually admitted by Baptists and paedobaptists alike that John baptized only upon condition of repentance (Matt. 3:6; Mark 1:4) unto the forgiveness of sins. Acts 19:4 reveals that John pointed men to Jesus as well. It is also clear that the disciples of Jesus baptized only those who were made disciples beforehand (John 4:1). There is no mention of, nor evidence for, infant baptism of the children of those who were made disciples in either John's or Jesus' baptisms. What, then, is the relationship between John's, Jesus', and Christian baptism? And what does the relationship have to say to us regarding paedobaptism?

One question that deals with this issue is this: who baptized Jesus' disciples into Christian baptism? It could not have been Jesus (John 4:1–2). John baptized at least Andrew and another disciple (John 1:35, 40), yet there is no record of their rebaptism by Jesus or by others at Pentecost. Apollos is another case of one of John's disciples of whom there is no record of rebaptism into Christian baptism (Acts 18:24–28). In fact, at Pentecost, only those conversing with Peter and who received his word were baptized (Acts 2:37–42). It appears that the disciples of Christ and the 120 in the upper room were not rebaptized into Christian baptism because it would have been repetitious for these believers to ask, "Brethren, what shall we do?" In fact, these 120 may have helped baptize the 3,000.

The only possible case for rebaptism in the New Testament is in Acts 19:1–7 (and Calvin disagrees). It seems that these disciples of John's baptism did not have the whole message of John about Jesus and the Holy Spirit when they were baptized. Perhaps they received it secondhand. Therefore, they were rebaptized into Christ by Paul. Calvin says that this rebaptism was not necessarily by water but by Christ's baptism with the Holy Spirit. He points to Paul's action of laying on hands and no mention of water to support his position. There is much disagreement on this text. But if we say John's baptism was not sufficient for Christian baptism, we still have the problems presented by Apollos' baptism, which was seemingly accepted by Aquila and Priscilla at Ephesus, and by the baptism of the faithful before Pentecost.

There does not seem to be a line of demarcation between John's, Jesus', and Christian baptism. This is further attested by the truth of Mark 1:1, which defines the beginning of the gospel of Jesus Christ with the coming of John in verse 2. Therefore, the subjects of John's and Jesus' gospel baptisms must apply also to Christian baptism; that is, the subjects are limited exclusively to disciples or professors. Jesus affirmed this in the Great Commission when He gave the command to make disciples of all the nations, baptizing and teaching "them" (Matt. 28:19). "Them" refers only to those who become disciples. Every use of the word "disciple" in the New Testament refers to a conscious, willful following of a teacher. When Christ commissioned His followers to baptize disciples, He was further establishing the practice of *believers' baptism*.

It might be added that Jesus clearly defined the basis for building His church in Matthew 16:16–19, 24–26 by means of the incident of Peter's confession. This is also a great support for the intended subjects of baptism into His church in the Great Commission. If we call baptism an institution by Christ for the outward sign of admission into His confessional church, should we not also trust His instituted precepts concerning the subjects of baptism rather than resorting to a very questionable reliance on "good and necessary inference?" It is my belief that Christ's instituted instructions for founding His church must interpret the application of the Abrahamic Covenant to baptism rather than vice versa by inference.

Some have tried to deny that Jesus defined confessors' baptism only in this text by claiming that His words refer exclusively to the initial institution of baptism. Therefore, the reasoning goes, we would expect a missionary-minded Christ to give instructions for confessors' baptism, naturally assuming the baptism of his/her infants to follow. However, the fact remains that Christ instituted baptism and practiced it Himself (through His disciples) long before the Great Commission (John 4:1). In His earlier baptism, He clearly baptized only those who were made disciples, excluding their infant children. If we are going to assume that the Great Commission is the official institution of Christian baptism, then was Christ's baptism not Christian? And why did He not add "baptizing them and their children?" The practice and command of Jesus' baptism, along with John's, names believers only as the subjects of baptism. I, for one, am not prepared to contradict either Christ's teaching or example.

I conclude, then, that John's, Jesus', and Christian baptisms are not to be artificially separated as has often been done. There is no good evidence of this pearl in Scripture and, therefore, no evidence that the subjects of baptism after Pentecost were any different from the subjects before. In both cases they were believing disciples.

7

THE SEVENTH PEARL

One of the most widely used arguments to support the practice of paedobaptism is its looming silence in the New Testament. The principal line of reasoning goes like this: It was so obviously a part of the covenant of grace to give covenant children the covenant sign in the Old Testament that there was no reason to mention or defend it in the New Testament. Thus, supposedly, the case is proven. However, this principle of hermeneutics which draws "good and necessary inferences" from silence can be quite subjective and can lead to error very quickly. It is, of course, a legitimate principle if there is no clear precept to contradict its inference. However, the regulative principle of Reformed worship requires positive institution for the sacraments.[12]

It is my contention that this argument for paedobaptism cannot stand when examined in the light of two major principles of hermeneutics: 1) the weight of regulative and instituted precept, and 2) ironically, the argument of silence itself when rightly employed.

Regulative Precept

Let us consider the weight of regulative precept. If we were to look for New Testament precepts for paedobaptism, our search would prove futile. As the great Presbyterian theologian B. B. Warfield said, "It is true that there is no express command to baptize infants in the New Testament, no express record of the baptism of infants, and no passages so stringently implying it that we must infer from them that infants were baptized."[13] The actual precepts concerning baptism can apply only to disciples because repentance and faith are necessary for New Covenant baptism. Many paedobaptists admit this much. However, the paedobaptist argument goes further to conclude that since these precepts are in the context of a missionary church, it is logical that there would only be calls to repentance and faith before baptism. Therefore, they say, the precepts for repentance and faith do not apply to infants of believers in an established church. For the paedobaptist, it would take an expressed precept to specifically prohibit infants from receiving the covenant sign of baptism because of the prior Abrahamic precept. Yet these same paedobaptists (i.e., Berkhof and Murray) quote the command to examine oneself as sufficient precept, along with the argument of silence concerning covenant communion, to prohibit unregenerate children of the Abrahamic Covenant who ate the Passover in the Old Testament from eating the Lord's Supper, which is the Passover's fulfillment in the New Testament.

This inconsistency in employing this prohibitive precept is exposed in the light of Acts 2:41–42, where all those baptized were permitted entrance to the breaking of bread, the Lord's Supper. If infant baptism is admitted in Acts 2, then so also must infant and small children's communion be admitted. It was many years later when the precepts of self-examination because of irreverent partaking were given. So in the paedobaptist position, there is confusion concerning the ground of entrance to the Lord's Supper-is it baptism or self-examination? And how shall the elders know to whom the Lord's Supper should be served if the primary ground is self-examination? In the light of these considerations, the precept of self-examination before partaking of the Lord's Supper (which is indeed legitimate) does not compare in strength to the precepts of repentance and faith before baptism. There is great inconsistency here and great danger in being arbitrarily selective in the application of these hermeneutic principles.

It appears that there is much more conclusive precept for excluding the infant children of believers from baptism than from the Lord's Supper. The precepts of confessors' baptism expressly prohibit infants from the covenant sign by their positive delineation of confessing subjects (Matt. 28:18–20). To let silence concerning infant baptism overpower the clear precepts of confessors' baptism is a dangerous hermeneutical method and a clear violation of the regulative principle of worship.

ARGUMENT OF SILENCE

In fact, if the argument of silence is applied consistently, there is even greater support for disciples' baptism. The council of Jerusalem in Acts 15 was called to deal with the Judaizers, who required circumcision for new Christians. The answer of the council concerning circumcision was that we are saved by grace alone without circumcision (15:11) and that it is good to "abstain from what has been sacrificed to idols, and from blood, and from what has been strangled, and from sexual immorality." If baptism is the direct counterpart of circumcision, then why did the council not simply say, "You and your children have been circumcised in the baptism of Christ and need not physical circumcision"? Here the argument of silence speaks against baptism as the direct counterpart of circumcision and in favor of salvation by grace or regeneration as its direct counterpart and abrogation (15:11).

Further, Paul wrote the entire letter of Galatians to deal with the Judaizers, who were requiring the Galatian church to be circumcised (Gal. 5:2–3). Why did Paul not simply say, "After believing, you and your children were baptized; thus, you have already received the New Covenant counterpart of circumcision and no longer need it?" Here again the argument of silence speaks against baptism as the direct counterpart of circumcision and speaks in favor of the receiving of the Spirit by hearing with faith as its counterpart and basis for abrogation. (Gal. 3:2–3).

An objection to this argument is that Paul would not allude to baptism as the reason for not receiving circumcision because that would put baptism in the class of works salvation like the Judaizers claimed for circumcision. I do not agree. Paul could easily have explained that neither circumcision nor baptism contribute to salvation in any way, yet water baptism is the fulfillment of circumcision, and it is no longer applicable in the New Covenant administration. But Paul did not do that. After clearly stating that circumcision has nothing to do with salvation, he explained that the new creation is the answer to the Judaizers for entrance into the true circumcision, the Israel of God (Gal. 6:15–16; Phil. 3:3). The whole teaching of Galatians is that it is not the children of the flesh and circumcision but the children of faith and regeneration who are the Israel of God and the true children of Abraham (Gal. 3:14, 29; 6:14–16). Thus, the argument of silence in the council and in Paul does not favor a New Covenant direct identity of circumcision with baptism and, therefore, neither does it in any way imply infant baptism.

Some have tried to legitimize the argument of silence for infant baptism by claiming a New Testament silence concerning, for example, the Christian Sabbath and the admission of women to the Lord's Supper. Yet the fourth commandment was taught by Jesus in the New Testament (Matt. 12; Mark 2), and there are explicit references to the

Lord's Day as being observed by Christians on the first day of the week (Acts 20:7; Rev. 1:10). There are also further correlating principles concerning the Ten Commandments for Christian practice (Rom. 2:14–15, 7:7, 8:4; Jer. 31:31–34). Further, concerning the admission of women to the Lord's Table, Paul clearly addresses both men and women in the first part of 1 Corinthians 11. When he goes on to discuss the responsibility to take the Lord's Supper properly he is still writing both to men and women. There is no such biblical evidence for infant baptism. In these two cases the argument of silence is not nearly as silent as in the case of infant baptism.

The argument of silence is certainly a hermeneutically legitimate principle but clear instruction overrules supposed logical inferences. People like John Murray would never follow such a hermeneutic on other matters. It is my conclusion that the "pearl" of silence is not good enough to string.

8

THE EIGHTH PEARL

THE ARGUMENT OF EXPANDED BLESSINGS

One of the great pearls that shines as brightly as the rest is found in rhetorical questions such as: If the Old Covenant children were granted the covenant sign, in this New Covenant day of expanded blessing and fulfillment, shall we prohibit the covenant sign to believers' children? Are our New Covenant children less blessed and privileged than were Old Covenant children? Such questions are certainly legitimate and lie at the heart of the matter of paedobaptism.

The primary power of such questions as an argument stems from the fact that no Christian wants to prohibit precious infants from God's blessings or to limit God's goodness in granting favor to infants. These thoughts tug at our heart-strings and constrain us to say "yes" to the covenant sign on our infants. However, God's Word, and not our well-intentioned sentimentality, must determine the answers to such questions as those in the above paragraph.

If God so chooses to grant physical children the covenant sign in the Old Covenant shadow and to prohibit the covenant sign to physical children in the New Covenant fulfillment, He has the sovereign right to do so. Nor does this necessarily imply that our New Covenant children are less privileged or blessed in being prohibited the New Covenant sign. I rhetorically reply: Are our children less blessed and privileged by being born to godly parents who show forth the fullness of the Spirit which was not fully outpoured in the Abrahamic Covenant? Are our children less blessed in having Christ and Him crucified proclaimed to them from infancy as compared to the types and shadows preached to their Old Testament counterparts? Are our children less privileged in being raised in the Israel of the Spirit as compared to the children raised in the Israel of the flesh? I think not.

Our children, above all others in the Old Covenant Israel and on the present-day earth, have privileges above measure. They are being raised in homes and churches which set the crucified and risen Lord of glory before them as their daily fare. Our gracious God has chosen them above multitudes that perish in gospel darkness to hear the same promise He sovereignly used to bring us into the everlasting kingdom:

Repent, and let every one of you be baptized in the name of Jesus Christ for the remission of sins; and you shall receive the gift of the Holy Spirit. For the promise [of the preceding sentence] is to you and to your children, and to all who are afar off, as many as [of you, your children, and all afar off] the Lord our God will call (Acts 2:38–39 NKJV).

Deut. 30:6 is an interesting passage in light of Acts 2:38ff and God's promise to circumcise the hearts of the Israelites and their offspring after He returns them from the prophesied exile. He seems to be referring to the same promise in Jeremiah 31:31–34 and Ezekiel 36:25ff. If we consider this passage to be fulfilled in the New Covenant administration of grace, we are rightly understanding Acts 2:38–39, 41 to say this:

> The promise of heart-circumcision is to you and your children, as many as the Lord our God shall call to Himself, as in the same case as the Gentiles. From your children God will circumcise hearts according to His sovereign calling and they may receive the sign of the New Covenant heart-circumcision on the basis of their outward repentance and faith (v. 41).

It does seem possible that God promises to call His elect out of believers' children as well as out of the Gentiles, but we cannot say that they are in the New Covenant of heart-circumcision and should receive its outward sign until they repent and believe. This concept of election from believers' "offspring" is akin to that of Hoeksema (*Believers and Their Seed*). Yet the precepts of baptism and the application of the New Covenant sign as illustrated in Acts 2:38–39, 41 prevent us from applying the sign of heart-circumcision until our children have shown evidence of having entered the New Covenant (Jer. 31:31–34).

Our children have been blessed with hearing and memorizing the written Word of God from the cradle. They have been blessed with the tear-stained prayers of Spirit-filled parents pleading for their souls' regeneration and conversion. They have been blessed with the New Covenant forms of the Old Covenant shadows to woo them to Christ. Can we say that they are less privileged in growing up under the sowed seed of the full revelation of God's sovereign plan? No! They cannot be considered less privileged when God has sovereignly chosen to preach the gospel of sovereign grace to them while so many of our fallen race perish each day in ignorance and darkness. Also, we have this promise of God to plead before Christ our personal Advocate for our children:

> So shall my word be that goes out from my mouth; it shall not return to me empty, but it shall accomplish that which I purpose, and shall succeed in the thing for which I sent it (Isa. 55:11).

Let us plead the goodness of God to His people and call down His Spirit to plant the Word of life in the hearts of our children till they bear the fruit of a new creation in Christ Jesus.

We Christians have every reason to say that our children have expanded blessings in the New Covenant – even if they, in God's good pleasure, must not receive the outward sign until they have a profession of faith. Let us not appeal to the shiny pearl of sentimental, rhetorical questions to set aside the revealed and chosen will of God in the New Covenant application of sovereign grace. Rather, let us proclaim the gospel of grace to our children, begging God for mercy upon them.

9

THE NINTH PEARL

Tradition is the last and smallest pearl which is threaded on the paedobaptist string. Too often in paedobaptist polemics, however, it is treated as if it were the largest. But if the Scripture is our only rule of faith and practice, then tradition's role must be only to clarify and corroborate what Scripture clearly sets forth. Two attractive areas of tradition are Jewish proselyte baptism and early church practice according to the apostolic fathers. In both of these traditions, T. E. Watson has presented the most incisive summary.

First of all, Edersheim and Berkhof both admit that Jewish proselytes and their children up to age twelve were baptized into Judaism.[14] However, unborn children in the womb of the baptized mother were not baptized after birth as they were considered already clean and a part of Israel. If we appeal to any part of the Judaistic practice, we have to contend with the late age of household children receiving baptism as well as the prohibition of baptism to unborn children in the womb. Neither of these difficulties lends any support to infant baptism. Some scholars discount Jewish proselyte baptism in the first century altogether. It is certainly no support for infant baptism.

Second, the very earliest explicit mention we have of infant baptism in the didactic writings of the early church is from Tertullian, around 200 A.D. In this passage he urges the delay of baptism, especially of little children, that its significance might be fully realized. This, of course, admits that little children or infants were being baptized in his day. But this is far from granting that it was an apostolic tradition.

Origen, Augustine, and many others following them say that it was the apostolic custom to baptize infants. It is probable that Origen was baptized as an infant ca. 185 A.D. He claims that this was the tradition handed down from the apostles. Irenaeus mentioned the stages of life from infancy to old age as the stages Christ went through to save all those who are born again at every age, thus possibly alluding to infant baptism via the tendency of the church fathers to identify baptism with regeneration. So it seems that from the second half of the second century to the Reformation in the sixteenth century, infant baptism was accepted as an apostolic tradition.

However, Irenaeus also claimed in his possible reference to baptism that he had received an apostolic tradition that Jesus was forty to fifty years old, contradicting the scriptural record. It is also well-known that the church fathers have claimed many other apostolic traditions that are unfounded. In fact, Tertullian is often recognized as a staunch defender of apostolic traditions. But why did he not defend infant baptism if it is an apostolic tradition? Such testimony must not be regarded as conclusive unless well-founded in Scripture.

Appeal can also be made to a much earlier source, namely the *Didache* (100–125 A. D.). This early church manual gives instruction only for the baptism of catechumens. Its silence on infant baptism is deafening. This is especially so because of the paedobaptist claim that the "missionary" church of Matthew 28:18–20 only recorded disciples' baptism at first, that infant baptism came later. But why then was infant baptism not mentioned in this church manual? As far as we know from Scripture and the *Didache*, it was not mentioned because it was not practiced.

The earliest clear didactic references to baptism are either silent about or negative toward infant baptism. I cannot let such uncertain evidence in tradition interpret Scripture or apostolic tradition for me. Tradition, as many paedobaptists agree, can offer corroborating proof only if infant baptism is first found in Scripture. Yet as I gaze through the eyes of Scripture, the small pearl of tradition shrinks in size and fades from sight.

CONCLUSION

A String Without Pearls

As I have examined each pearl on the string, I have come away with, at best, a necklace of discolored and missing jewels. In reality, I confess that I am left with an empty string called "good and necessary inference" which does me no good in showing the beauty of Christian baptism. It is a string of twine around the neck of a princess.

I cannot build my doctrine on an empty string. Therefore, I accept the one priceless pearl of disciples' baptism and wear it upon my hand as a sign of my marriage to Christ. Baptism is the outward sign of entrance into the New Covenant by the inward circumcision of the heart, evidenced by one's confession of faith in Christ. Old Testament children entered the Abrahamic Covenant by the circumcision of the flesh. If they came to faith, it became a seal of the righteousness of faith, as it was to Abraham (Rom. 4). Now our New Covenant children enter the New Covenant by the circumcision of the heart, sealed by the Holy Spirit and signified by the sign of disciples' baptism.

I rejoice to see a revival of Reformed beliefs in our Baptist churches across the land. Baptists are rediscovering their Reformed roots. However, the work of restoring biblical truth has cost many pastors their jobs and their families' peace of mind. In love, I challenge those with Baptist convictions not to accept too quickly a welcome refuge in paedobaptist churches. Stand fast with Baptists to "strengthen the things that remain" instead of fleeing to what appears to be more welcome surroundings.

It is sad to see Baptist pastors and laymen gloss over baptism in order to serve in paedobaptist churches. Before any such change is contemplated, God's Word should be studied on the subject with diligence and honesty. Pastors take vows on such things. Baptists today need sacrificial Luthers, Calvins, and Bunyans in our pulpits and pews to count the cost of building biblically Reformed and baptistic churches of faithful disciples. It ought to be done. It can be done. And by God's grace, it is being done with increasing frequency all over the world.

Finally, having gone through so many struggles on the question of Christian baptism, I can only heartily plead for unity and understanding between Baptists and paedobaptist brethren who hold the great doctrines of grace in common – to God's glory in His church.

Selected Bibliography

Baillie, John, John T. McNeill, and Henry P. Van
      Dusen, eds. *The Library of Christian Classics*.
      Vol. XX-XXI, *Calvin: Institutes of the Christian
      Religion*, by John Calvin. Translated by Ford Lewis
      Battles. Philadelphia: Westminster Press, 1960.

Berkhof, L. *Systematic Theology*. Grand Rapids: William
B. Eerdmans, 1941.

Hoeksema, Herman. *Believers and Their Seed*. Grand
      Rapids: Reformed Free Publishing Asso., 1971.

Jewett, Paul K. *Infant Baptism & the Covenant of Grace*.
      Grand Rapids: William B. Eerdmans, 1978.

Kingdon, David, *Children of Abraham*. Sussex, England:
Carey Publications 1973.

Kline, Meredith G. *By Oath Consigned*. Grand Rapids:
William B. Eerdmans, 1968.

Marcel, Pierre Ch. *The Biblical Doctrine of Infant Baptism*.
      Translated by Philip Edgcumbe Hughes. London:
      James Clarke & Co., 1953.

Marston, George. *Are You a Biblical Baptist?* Pamphlet.

Murray, John. *Christian Baptism*. Philadelphia: Presbyterian & Reformed Pub. Co., 1970.

Ridderbos, Herman. *The Coming of the Kingdom*. Philadelphia: Presbyterian & Reformed Pub. Co., 1962.

Robertson, O. Palmer. *The Christ of the Covenants*. Phillipsburg, NJ: Presbyterian & Reformed Pub. Co., 1980.

Watson, T. E., *Should Infants Be Baptized?* Grand Rapids: Guardian Press, 1962.

Warfield, B. B., *Studies in Theology*. Oxford University Press, 1932. Reprint edition, Baker Book House: Grand Rapids, 1981.

Scripture Index

New Testament (cont.)

ENDNOTES

[1] *Westminster Confession of Faith*, 21.1; *Second London Baptist Confession*, 22.1.

[2] John Calvin, The *Institutes of the Christian Religion,* eds. John Baillie, John T. McNeill, and Henry P. Van Dusen, trans. Ford Lewis Battles (Philadelphia: Westminster Press, 1960), 4.15.19.

[3] L. Berkhof, *Systematic Theology* (Grand Rapids: William B. Eerdmans, 1941), 656.

[4] John Murray, *Christian Baptism* (Philadelphia: Presbyterian & Reformed Pub. Co., 1970) 76–79.

[5] Murray, 72.

[6] Meredith G. Kline, *By Oath Consigned* (Grand Rapids: William B. Eerdmans, 1968), 94–102.

[7] Kline, 98.

[8] Walt Chantry, "Baptism and Covenant Theology" (The Reformed Reader, 1999).

[9] Herman Ridderbos, *The Coming of the Kingdom* (Philadelphia: Presbyterian & Reformed Pub. Co., 1962), 202.

[10] see George Marston, "Are You a Biblical Baptist?", 21–22.

[11] Kline, *By Oath Consigned*, 94–102.

[12] see WCF 20.5.

[13] B. B. Warfield, *Studies in Theology* (1932; repr., Grand Rapids: Baker Book House, 1981), 399.

[14] Alfred Edersheim, *Life and Times of Jesus the Messiah*, Updated Ed. (Carol Stream, IL: Hendrickson Publishing Group, 1993), 746; Berkhof, *Systematic Theology*, 622.

FOUNDERS
M I N I S T R I E S

Founders Ministries exists for the recovery of the gospel
and the reformation of churches.

We have been providing resources for churches since 1982 through
conferences, books, The Sword & The Trowel Podcast, video
documentaries, online articles found at www.founders.org, the quarterly
Founders Journal, Bible studies, International church search, and the
seminary level training program, the Institute of Public Theology.
Founders believes that the biblical faith is inherently doctrinal, and we are
therefore confessional in our convictions.

You can learn more about Founders Ministries and how to partner with
us at www.founders.org.

FoundersMin

FoundersMin

FoundersMinistries

FoundersMinistries

OTHER TITLES FROM FOUNDERS PRESS

Truth & Grace Memory Books

Edited by Thomas K. Ascol

> Memorizing a good, age-appropriate catechism is as
> valuable for learning the Bible as memorizing multi-
> plication tables is for learning mathematics.
>
> —Dr. Don Whitney, Professor,
> The Southern Baptist Theological Seminary

Dear Timothy: Letters on Pastoral Ministry

Edited by Thomas K. Ascol

> Get this book. So many experienced pastors have written in this
> book it is a gold mine of wisdom for young pastors in how to preach
> and carry out their ministerial life.
>
> —Joel Beeke, President,
> Puritan Reformed Theological Seminary

The Mystery of Christ, His Covenant & His Kingdom

By Samuel Renihan

> This book serves for an excellent and rich primer on covenant
> theology and demonstrates how it leads from the Covenant of
> Redemption to the final claiming and purifying of the people given
> by the Father to the Son.
>
> —Tom Nettles, Retired Professor of Historical Theology,
> The Southern Baptist Theological Seminary

By WHAT STANDARD? God's World . . . God's Rules.

Edited by Jared Longshore

I'm grateful for the courage of these men and the clarity of their voices. This is a vitally important volume, sounding all the right notes of passion, warning, instruction, and hope.

—Phil Johnson,
Executive Director of Grace To You

Strong And Courageous: Following Jesus Amid the Rise of America's New Religion

By Tom Ascol and Jared Longshore

We have had quite enough of "Be Nice and Inoffensive." We are overflowing with "Be Tolerant and Sensitive." It is high time that we were admonished to "Be Strong and Courageous."

—Jim Scott Orrick, Author,
Pastor of Bullitt Lick Baptist Church